BIBLE & BOOK OF MORMON ACTIVITY BOOK

For Latter-day Saint Kids

CRACK THE CO

KEY

A B C D E F G H I

N O P Q R S T U V

HELP DECODE MORONI'S MESSAGE

SPOT THE DIFFERENCES

SPOT THE SIX DIFFERENCE BETWEEN THE TWO PICTURES. CIRCLE DIFFERENCES IN BOTTOM PICTURE.

MOSES

R O N X O S K
N N A L D W Y
O S E S M G A
A E L I T E S
X Y L R Z J P
F R E E U Y S
D E R N E S S
I I K S E A Q
A R A O H D
H E T H C P
ARAOH   ISRAELITES
WILDERNESS
PROPHET

Nearly 130 pages of fun activities!

THIS BOOK BELONGS TO:

_____

HOW MANY DO YOU COUNT?

YOUR ANSWER ☐

HOW MANY BIBLES DO YOU COUNT?

TIC-TAC-TOE

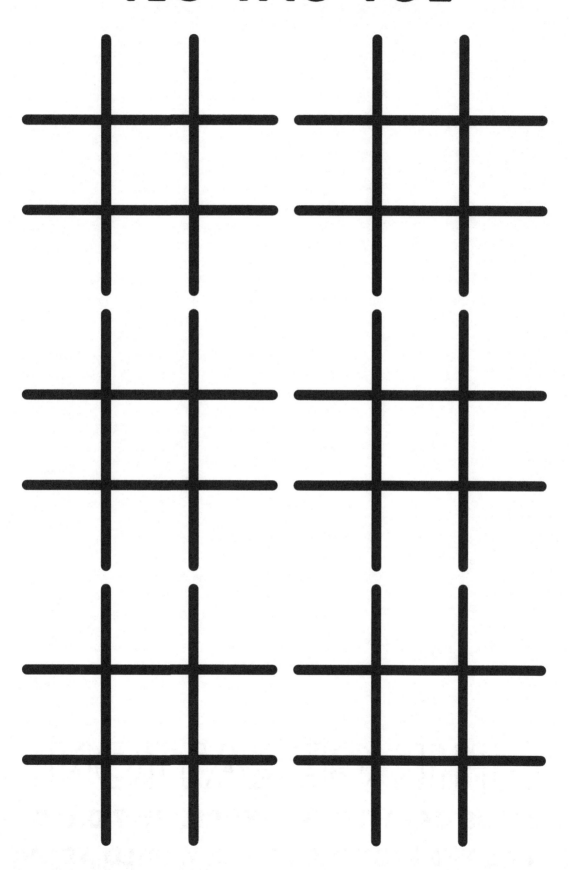

PLAYER ONE___　　　　　　　**PLAYER TWO___**

TRACE IT

THE CREATION

**JESUS CREATED THE WORLD IN 7 DAYS.
TRACE THE PICTURE OF THE WORLD ABOVE.**

FIND THE MATCH

CAN YOU FIND WHICH TWO WORLDS EXACTLY MATCH?
CIRCLE THE PICTURES THAT MATCH.

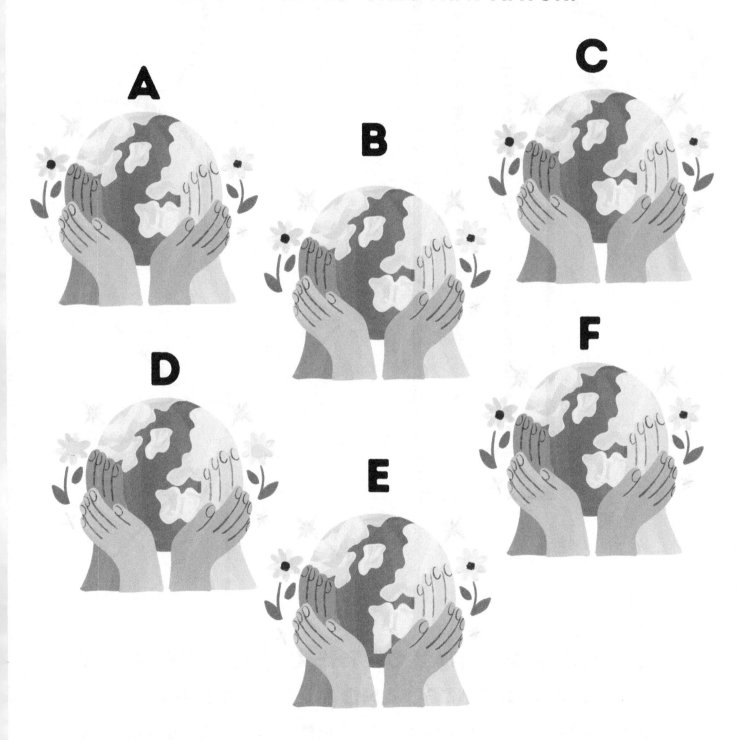

ON THE FIRST DAY OF THE CREATION LIGHT WAS CREATED AND DIVIDED FROM DARKNESS. COMPLETE THE MAZE STARTING AT "S" AND FINISHING AT "F" & COLOR THE PICTURES.

GOD SAW THAT IT WAS GOOD

HOW MANY WORDS CAN YOU MAKE USING THE LETTERS FROM WORDS ABOVE "GOD SAW THAT IT WAS GOOD"?

_____   _____

_____   _____

_____   _____

_____   _____

_____   _____

_____   _____

_____   _____

_____   _____

_____

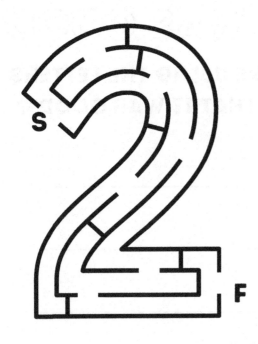

ON THE SECOND DAY OF
THE CREATION THE CLOUDS
& OCEANS WERE CREATED.
COMPLETE THE MAZE &
COLOR THE PICTURES.

SPOT THE DIFFERENCES

CAN YOU SPOT THE SIX DIFFERENCES BETWEEN THE TOP AND BOTTOM PICTURES? CIRCLE THE SIX DIFFERENCES IN THE BOTTOM PICTURE.

S

F

ON THE THIRD DAY OF THE CREATION THE DRY LAND & VEGETATION WAS CREATED. COMPLETE THE MAZE & COLOR THE PICTURES.

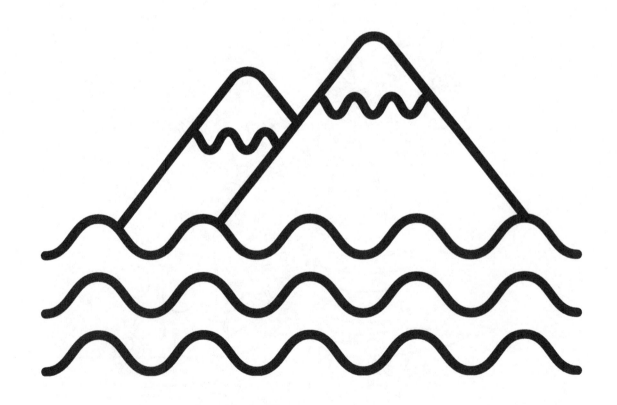

ON THE FOURTH DAY OF THE CREATION THE STARS, MOON, & SUN WERE CREATED. COMPLETE THE MAZE & COLOR THE PICTURES.

```
A  D  A  M  B  J  C  V  M  K
R  F  R  U  I  T  R  N  G  Q
E  E  D  B  A  G  E  N  C  Y
R  M  T  L  Q  D  A  P  D  Z
S  T  N  S  R  Y  T  H  Z  V
E  H  I  A  V  Q  I  P  N  J
K  D  G  T  X  S  O  P  Z  O
E  V  E  A  P  V  N  N  S  Y
X  Y  S  N  Q  L  T  R  E  E
D  Y  Z  L  K  Y  V  L  P  Y
```

ADAM & EVE

ADAM	EVE	CREATION
GARDEN	EDEN	TREE
SATAN	FRUIT	AGENCY
JOY		

COMPLETE THE WORD SEARCH ABOVE TO FIND THE WORDS RELATED TO THE GARDEN OF EDEN.

ON THE FIFTH DAY OF THE CREATION BIRDS & FISHES OF THE SEA WERE CREATED. COMPLETE THE MAZE & COLOR THE PICTURES.

ON THE SIXTH DAY OF THE
CREATION LAND CREATURES
& MAN WERE CREATED.
COMPLETE THE MAZE &
COLOR THE PICTURES.

YOU ARE CREATED IN GOD'S IMAGE

DRAW A PICTURE OF YOURSELF & THEN WRITE THREE THINGS YOU LIKE TO DO BELOW.

1. _____
2. _____
3. _____

HIDDEN PICTURES

FIND THE PICTURES BELOW HIDDEN INSIDE THE PICTURE AND COLOR THEM WHEN YOU FIND THEM.

ON THE SEVENTH DAY
OF THE CREATION GOD
RESTED & BLESSED IT.
COMPLETE THE MAZE &
COLOR THE PICTURES.

TIC-TAC-TOE

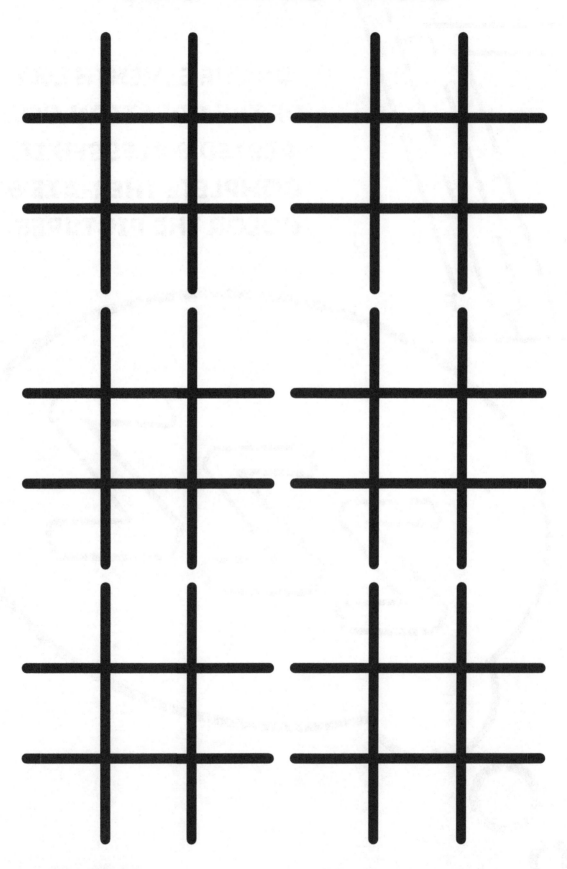

PLAYER ONE___   **PLAYER TWO___**

COLOR NOAH'S ARK & DRAW ANIMALS ON THE ARK.

WHICH PATH?

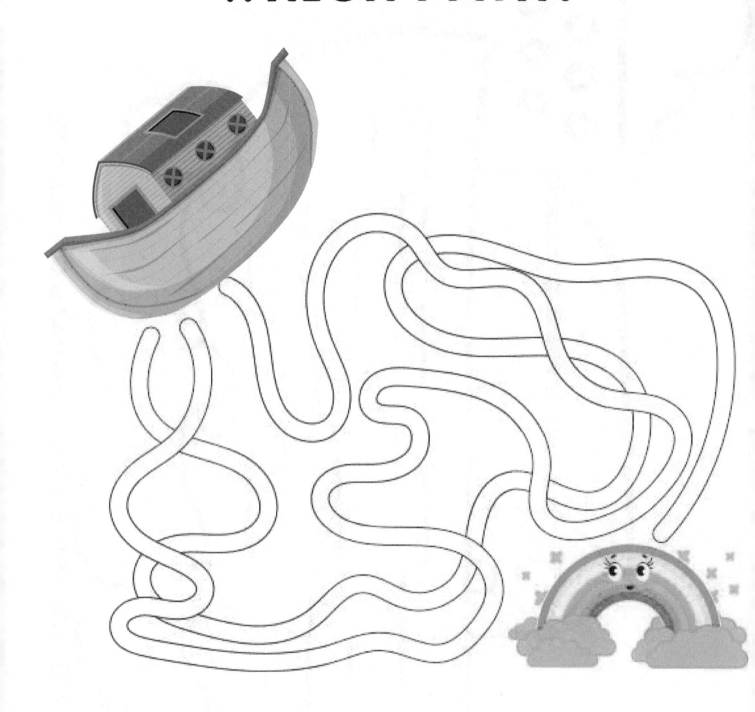

WHICH PATH SHOULD NOAH'S ARK TAKE TO GET TO THE RAINBOW?

S	F	B	X	T	M	F	Y	A	G
W	C	S	V	P	F	L	B	N	F
I	J	O	J	H	I	O	C	I	U
C	S	D	F	M	M	O	K	M	R
K	H	W	A	I	H	D	I	A	A
E	H	F	R	A	I	N	I	L	I
D	D	N	O	L	O	E	J	S	N
X	O	N	X	E	V	Q	K	T	B
D	V	O	T	A	T	R	W	K	O
J	E	O	L	F	A	O	S	F	W

NOAH

NOAH	ARK	RAIN
FLOOD	ANIMALS	WICKED
FAMILY	DOVE	LEAF
RAINBOW		

COMPLETE THE WORD SEARCH ABOVE TO FIND THE WORDS RELATED TO NOAH'S ARK.

SPOT THE DIFFERENCES

CAN YOU FIND THE DIFFERENCE BETWEEN THE TWO PICTURES OF NOAH'S ARK ABOVE? CIRCLE THE SIX DIFFERENCES IN THE BOTTOM PICTURE.

TIC-TAC-TOE

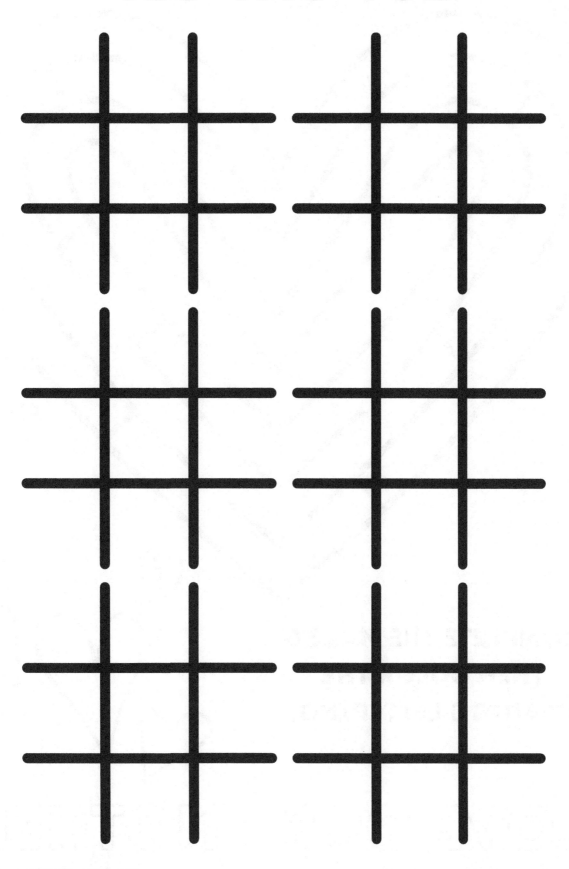

PLAYER ONE___ **PLAYER TWO___**

START

FINISH

COMPLETE THE MAZE &
THEN COLOR THE
HEARTS & LETTERING.

LOVE ONE ANOTHER

HIDDEN PICTURES

FIND THE PICTURES LISTED BELOW HIDDEN INSIDE THE PICTURE
AND COLOR THEM WHEN YOU FIND THEM.

NOAH SENT A DOVE OUT TO SEE IF THE FLOOD WAS OVER. THE DOVE RETURNED WITH AN OLIVE LEAF IN ITS BEAK, SO HE KNEW THE FLOOD WAS FINISHED. GOD GAVE THE SIGN OF THE RAINBOW AS A PROMISE THAT HE WILL NEVER FLOOD THE WHOLE EARTH AGAIN. COLOR THE PICTURE BELOW.

I LIKE TO LOOK FOR RAINBOWS WHENEVER THERE IS RAIN.

COMPLETE THE MAZE & THEN WRITE THE NAMES OF SOME PEOPLE YOU LOVE IN THE HEARTS.

TRACE IT

NOAH WAS OBEDIENT

TRACE NOAH'S ARK ABOVE.

Moses

COLOR MOSES PARTING THE RED SEA.

TIC-TAC-TOE

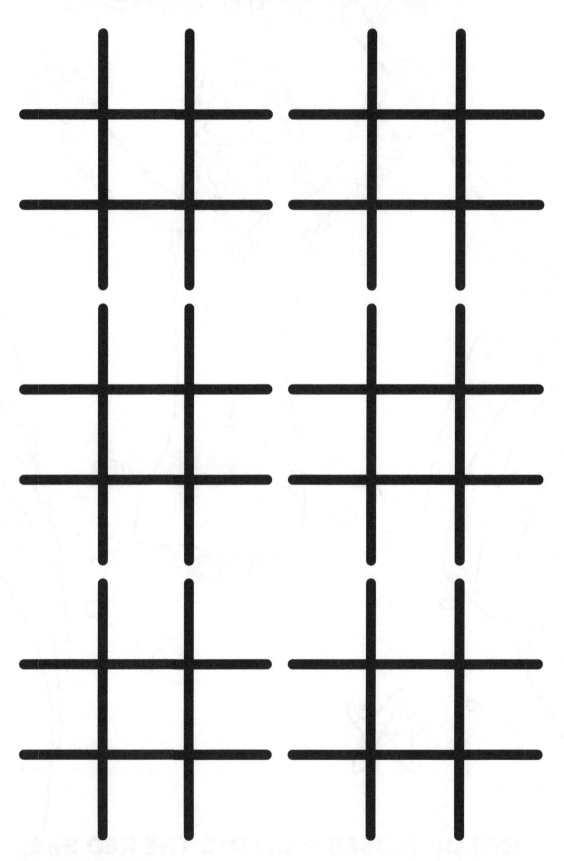

PLAYER ONE___   **PLAYER TWO___**

MOSES LEADING THE ISRAELITES

Start

Finish

FIND YOUR WAY THROUGH THE MAZE AND HELP MOSES LEAD THE ISRAELITES TO THE PROMISED LAND.

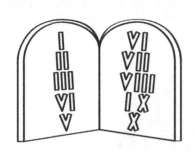

MATCH EACH COMMANDMENT WITH THE PICTURE THAT REPRESENTS THAT COMMANDMENT.

You should have no other gods before Me.

You should make no idols.

You should not take the name of the Lord your God in vain.

Keep the Sabbath day holy.

Honor your father and your mother.

You should not murder.

You should not commit adultery.

You should not steal.

You should not bear false witness against your neighbor.

You should not covet.

HIDDEN PICTURES

FIND THE PICTURES LISTED BELOW HIDDEN INSIDE THE PICTURE ABOVE AND COLOR THEM WHEN YOU FIND THEM.

```
H  A  A  R  O  N  X  O  S  K
M  M  A  N  N  A  L  D  W  Y
Q  R  M  O  S  E  S  M  G  A
I  S  R  A  E  L  I  T  E  S
G  Q  P  X  Y  L  R  Z  J  P
J  D  U  F  R  E  E  U  Y  S
W  I  L  D  E  R  N  E  S  S
C  F  O  H  I  K  S  E  A  Q
C  F  P  H  A  R  A  O  H  D
P  R  O  P  H  E  T  H  C  P
```

MOSES

MOSES	PHARAOH	ISRAELITES
FREE	SEA	WILDERNESS
MANNA	AARON	PROPHET

COMPLETE THE WORD SEARCH ABOVE TO FIND THE WORDS RELATED TO THE STORY OF MOSES.

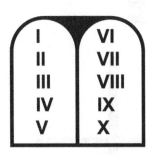

MAKE YOUR WAY THROUGH THE MAZE AND SEE HOW FOLLOWING THE COMMANDMENTS LEADS YOU TO JOY.

Start

joy

TIC-TAC-TOE

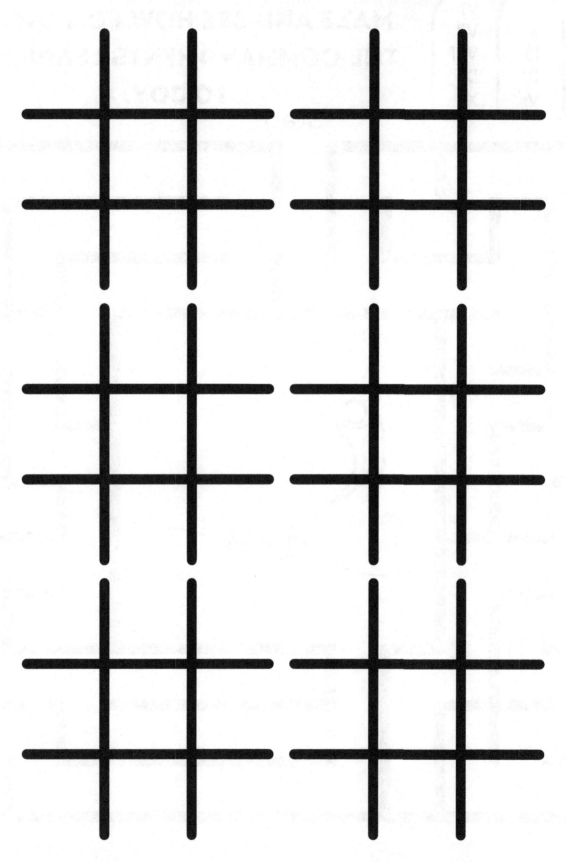

PLAYER ONE___   **PLAYER TWO___**

JACOB HAD TWELVE SONS, WHO BECAME THE 12 TRIBES OF ISRAEL. JOSEPH'S HOUSE CONTAINED THE TRIBES OF EPHRAIM & MANASSEH. COLOR EACH OF THE BROTHERS BELOW.

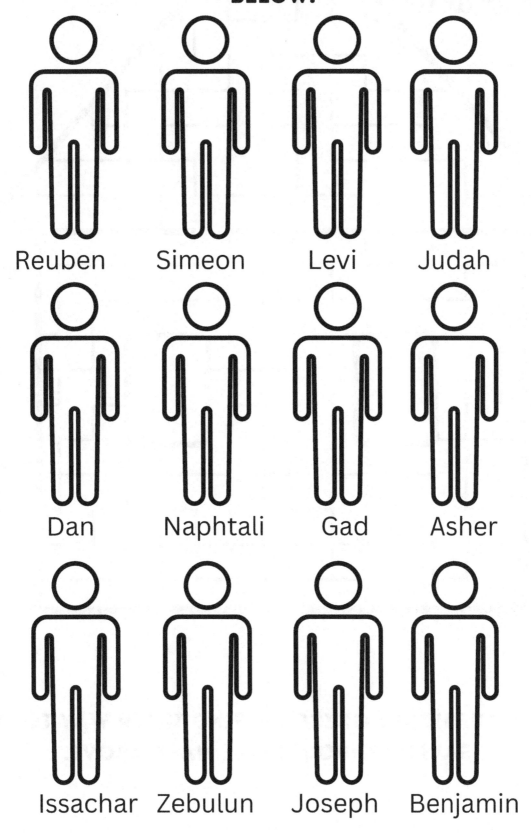

Reuben Simeon Levi Judah

Dan Naphtali Gad Asher

Issachar Zebulun Joseph Benjamin

HELP THE HOUSE OF ISRAEL FIND THEIR WAY TO THE SAVIOR THROUGH THE MAZE ABOVE.

CRACK THE CODE

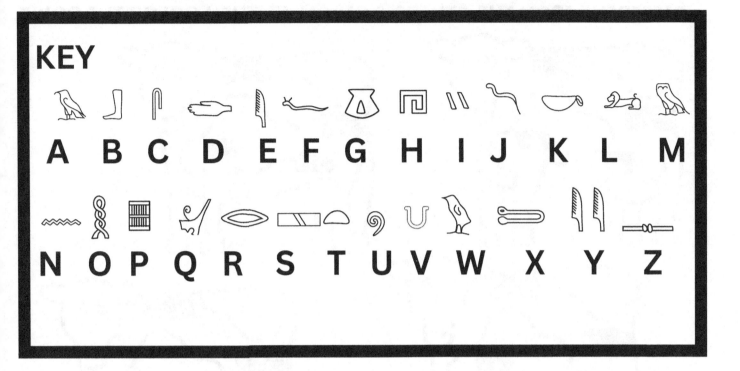

KEY

A	B	C	D	E	F	G	H	I	J	K	L	M

N	O	P	Q	R	S	T	U	V	W	X	Y	Z

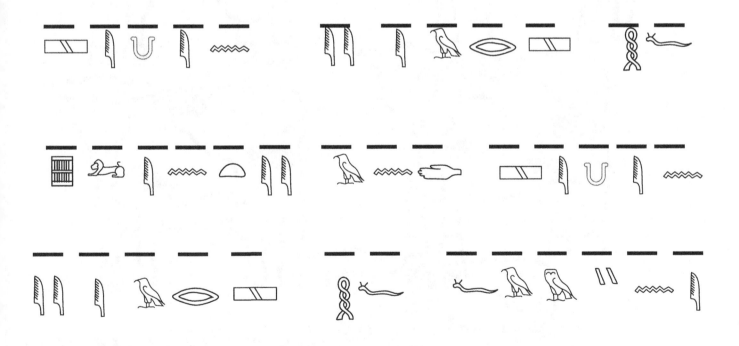

SEVEN YEARS OF

PLENTY AND SEVEN

YEARS OF FAMINE

JOSEPH INTERPRETED PHARAOH'S DREAM. HELP UNLOCK THE CODE TO FIND OUT THE MEANING OF THE DREAM USING THE KEY ABOVE.

JOSEPH INTERPRETED PHARAOH'S DREAM. THE SEVEN FAT COWS REPRESENTED SEVEN YEARS OF PLENTY. FIND THE COW THAT IS DIFFERENT FROM THE OTHERS & CIRCLE IT. THEN COLOR THE COWS.

WHICH ONE IS DIFFERENT?

```
O  Z  C  U  Q  H  R  I  P  T
B  S  O  N  S  D  E  L  B  P
F  L  A  O  O  R  U  G  H  H
J  A  T  U  L  E  N  C  J  C
Z  O  M  N  D  A  I  F  R  H
E  F  S  I  W  M  T  K  J  U
G  B  L  E  N  S  E  S  A  K
Y  M  G  P  P  E  D  L  C  Q
P  O  T  I  P  H  A  R  O  T
T  A  T  L  Q  A  J  D  B  D
```

JOSEPH

JACOB	SONS	JOSEPH
COAT	SOLD	EGYPT
POTIPHAR	DREAMS	FAMINE
REUNITED		

COMPLETE THE WORD SEARCH ABOVE TO FIND THE WORDS RELATED TO THE STORY OF JOSEPH.

TIC-TAC-TOE

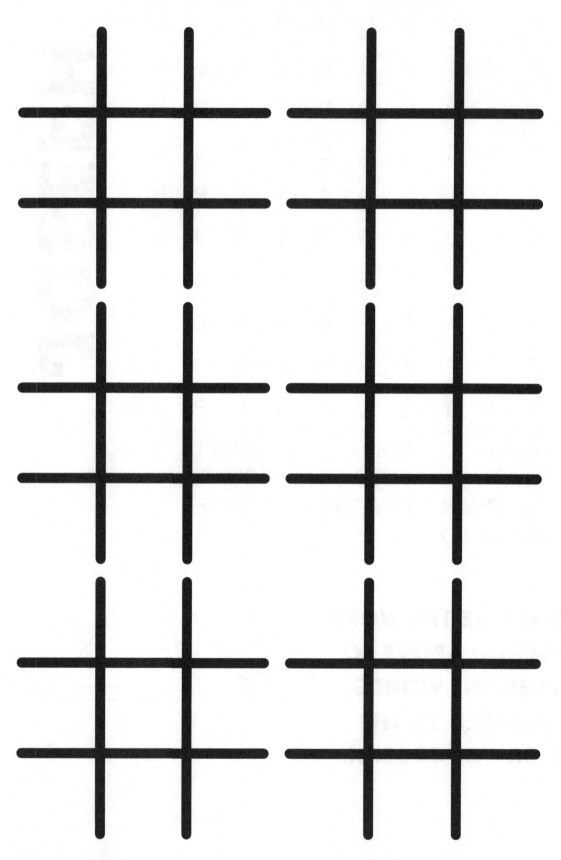

PLAYER ONE____   **PLAYER TWO____**

I CAN BE COURAGEOUS LIKE DAVID

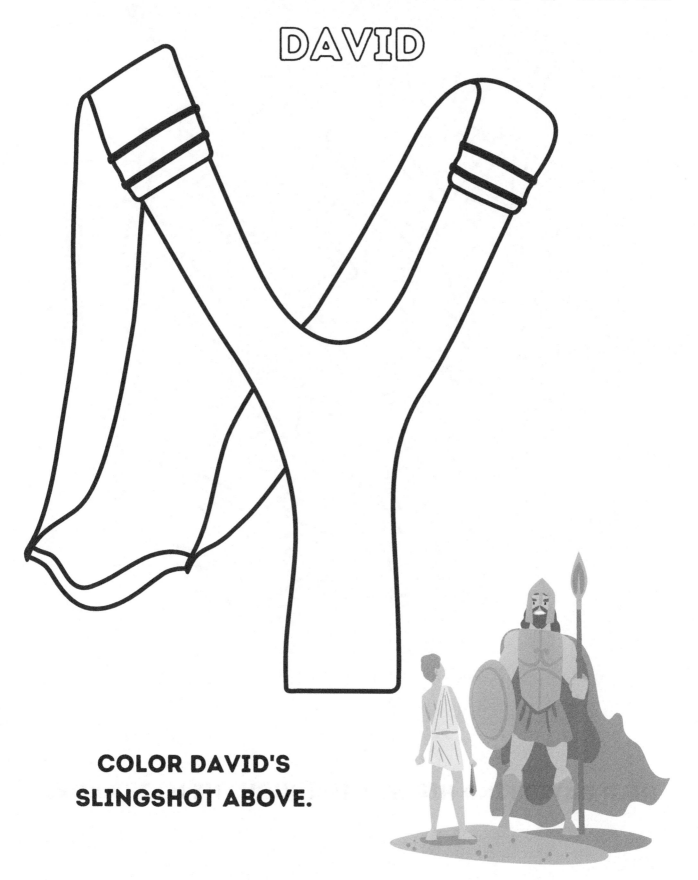

**COLOR DAVID'S
SLINGSHOT ABOVE.**

HELP DAVID FIND HIS WAY THROUGH THE MAZE ABOVE.

```
C  C  S  V  M  N  D  O  G  S
X  C  U  O  Z  I  Z  M  Y  H
E  L  I  N  V  J  H  F  S  E
M  T  B  A  T  T  L  E  K  E
I  I  D  U  A  J  V  V  I  P
E  N  S  I  M  S  L  I  N  G
E  L  L  T  W  C  G  G  G  E
S  O  A  T  A  S  T  O  N  E
G  K  C  T  P  K  Z  R  E  D
R  E  P  E  N  T  E  D  S  G
```

DAVID

DAVID	SHEEP	GOLIATH
SLING	STONE	KING
MISTAKE	BATTLE	REPENTED

COMPLETE THE WORD SEARCH ABOVE TO FIND THE WORDS RELATED TO THE STORY OF DAVID.

TIC-TAC-TOE

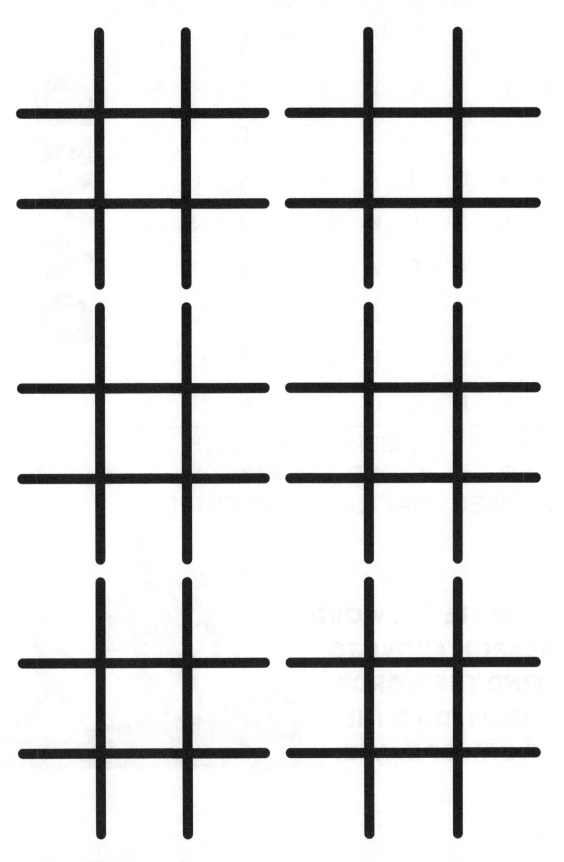

PLAYER ONE___   **PLAYER TWO___**

SPOT THE DIFFERENCES

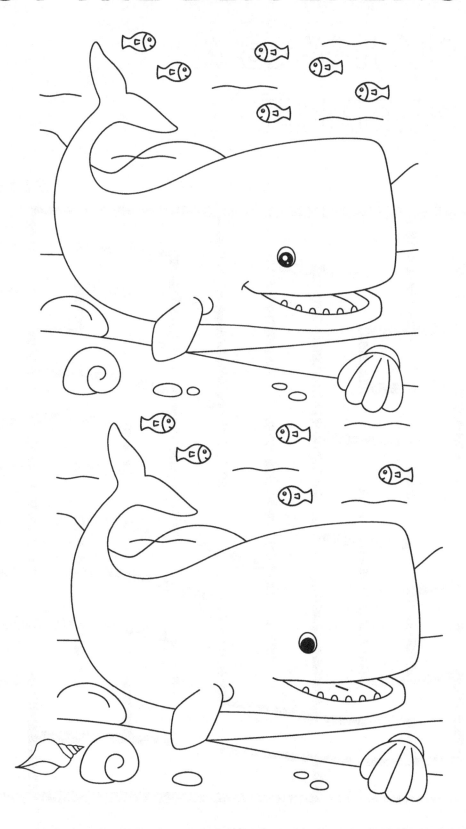

JONAH WAS SWALLOWED BY A WHALE AND WAS INSIDE FOR NEARLY THREE DAYS. CAN YOU FIND THE DIFFERENCES BETWEEN THE TWO PICTURES ABOVE? CIRCLE THE SIX DIFFERENCES IN THE BOTTOM PICTURE.

JONAH WAS A PROPHET

START

FINISH

HELP JONAH FIND HIS WAY THROUGH THE MAZE ABOVE.

```
I  I  W  H  A  L  E  T  D  X
W  G  P  N  I  N  E  V  E  H
M  G  Z  F  S  H  I  P  N  K
I  K  T  H  R  O  W  N  I  T
R  J  S  W  A  L  L  O  W  L
E  U  O  A  L  B  E  L  L  Y
P  Y  D  N  R  E  P  E  N  T
E  M  X  E  A  O  C  P  C  F
N  F  F  R  I  H  K  H  E  N
T  O  D  C  S  T  O  R  M  O
```

JONAH

JONAH   NINEVEH   REPENT
SHIP   STORM   THROWN
SWALLOW   WHALE   BELLY
REPENT

COMPLETE THE WORD SEARCH ABOVE TO FIND THE WORDS RELATED TO THE STORY OF JONAH.

HOW MANY DO YOU COUNT?

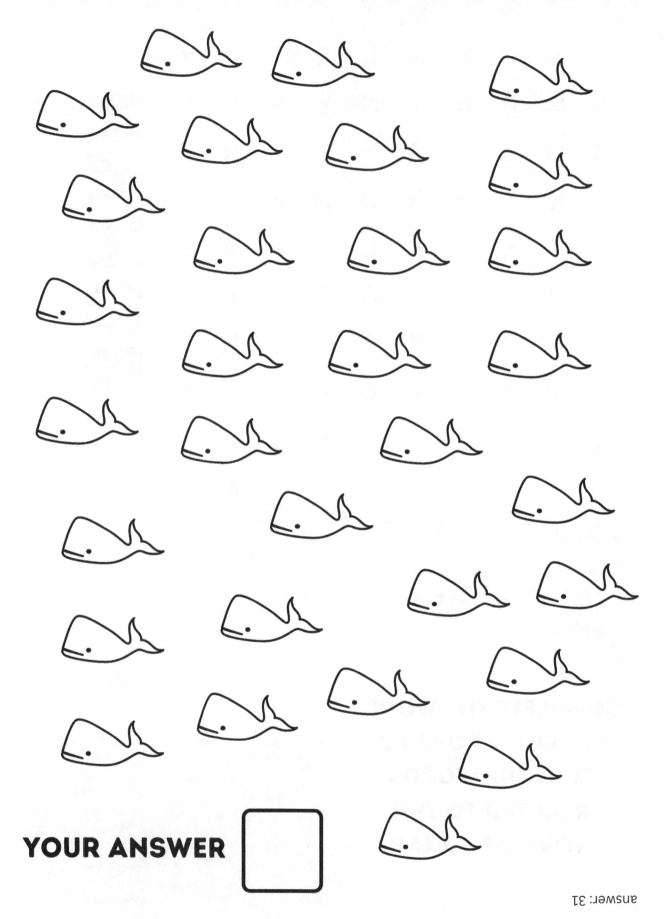

YOUR ANSWER

TIC-TAC-TOE

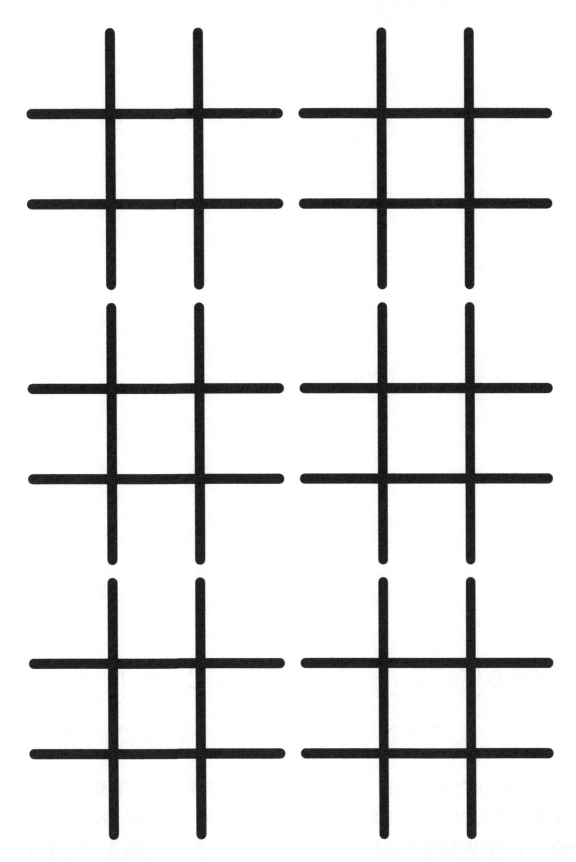

PLAYER ONE___   **PLAYER TWO___**

TRACE IT

SHADRACH, MESHACH, AND ABEDNEGO WERE COURAGEOUS

SHADRACH, MESHACH, AND ABEDNEGO WERE THROWN INTO A FIERY FURNACE FOR REFUSING TO BOW TO AN IMAGE OF THE KING. THEY WERE NOT HARMED. TRACE THE FLAMES ABOVE.

WHICH ONE IS DIFFERENT?

DANIEL WAS THROWN INTO A DEN OF LIONS FOR PRAYING, WHICH WASN'T ALLOWED UNDER A NEW LAW. WHICH OF THE LION'S ABOVE IS DIFFERENT FROM THE OTHERS? CIRCLE THE THING THAT IS DIFFERENT AND THEN COLOR THE LIONS.

DANIEL WAS FAITHFUL

HEAVENLY FATHER LOVES HEARING FROM YOU THROUGH PRAYER. FIND YOUR WAY TO THE SMILE IN THE MIDDLE OF THE MAZE.

```
U  R  I  S  A  V  E  D  Q  I
R  M  F  U  R  N  A  C  E  N
I  Q  O  T  U  R  Q  V  B  R
D  H  L  I  O  N  S  Q  C  Q
O  N  D  T  K  I  N  G  D  I
L  E  N  R  W  C  B  E  B  S
F  A  S  T  E  D  F  Z  B  B
V  L  T  P  R  A  Y  E  R  H
T  C  C  F  S  S  M  X  N  F
G  Q  D  A  N  I  E  L  T  K
```

DANIEL

KING	DANIEL	DREAM
IDOL	FURNACE	SAVED
PRAYER	LIONS	FASTED
SAFE		

COMPLETE THE WORD SEARCH ABOVE TO FIND THE WORDS RELATED TO THE STORY OF DANIEL.

TIC-TAC-TOE

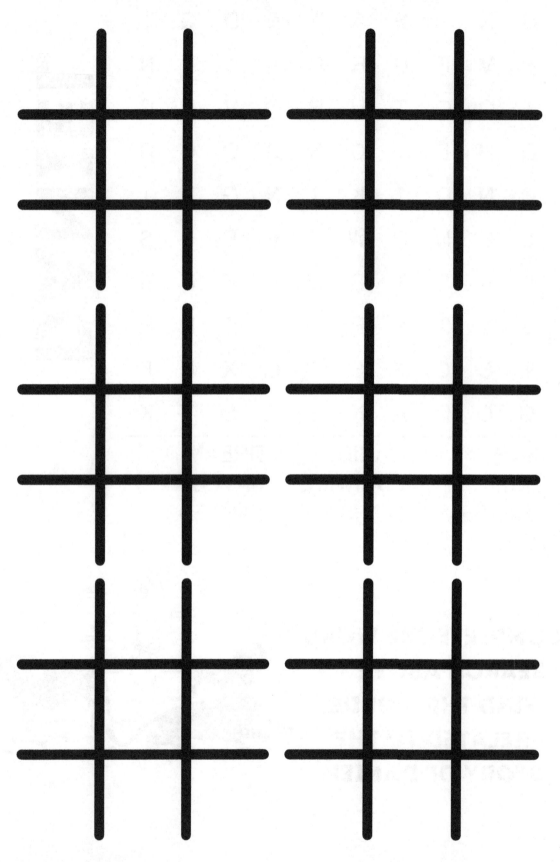

PLAYER ONE___   **PLAYER TWO___**

I CAN BE BRAVE LIKE ESTHER

QUEEN ESTHER WAS BRAVE & APPROACHED THE KING WITHOUT BEING
INVITED TO ASK HIM TO SAVE THE JEWISH PEOPLE. SHE COULD HAVE BEEN
KILLED FOR APPROACHING THE KING WITHOUT AN INVITE, BUT SHE
FASTED & PRAYED BEFORE GOING TO HIM & HAD FAITH HE WOULD LISTEN.
COLOR THE PICTURE BELOW OF ESTHER.

START

FINISH

ESTHER LOVED HER PEOPLE & WANTED TO SAVE THEM.
MAKE YOUR WAY THROUGH THE "LOVE" MAZE ABOVE.

RHYME TIME

ESTHER ASKED THE JEWS TO FAST FOR HER BEFORE SHE WENT TO SEE THE KING UNANNOUNCED. CIRCLE OR COLOR THE WORD BUBBLES BELOW THAT RHYME WITH "FAST".

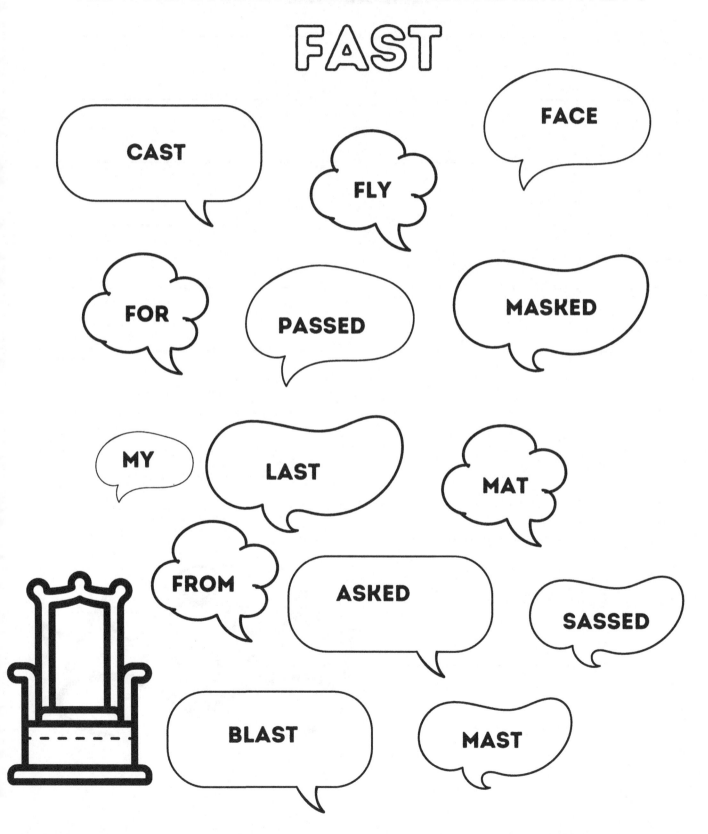

BORN FOR SUCH A TIME AS THIS

HOW MANY WORDS CAN YOU MAKE USING THE LETTERS FROM THE SCRIPTURE IN ESTHER 4:14 "BORN FOR SUCH A TIME AS THIS"?

_____   _____

_____   _____

_____   _____

_____   _____

_____   _____

_____   _____

_____   _____

_____

_____

_____

_____

```
A I K Y F Q H N A D
M F P S M Z A F A B
M X Q R H M T R N G
J I I U A Q E G K E
E K G H E Y D D F S
W F A S T E D D D T
S H D Z V G N E K H
N D P A N Y V A I E
A D R I I A C B L R
N B K K S A H Y L I
```

ESTHER   KING   QUEEN
HAMAN   HATED   JEWS
KILL   FASTED   PRAY
BRAVE   SAVED

COMPLETE THE WORD SEARCH ABOVE TO FIND THE WORDS RELATED TO THE STORY OF ESTHER.

ESTHER

TIC-TAC-TOE

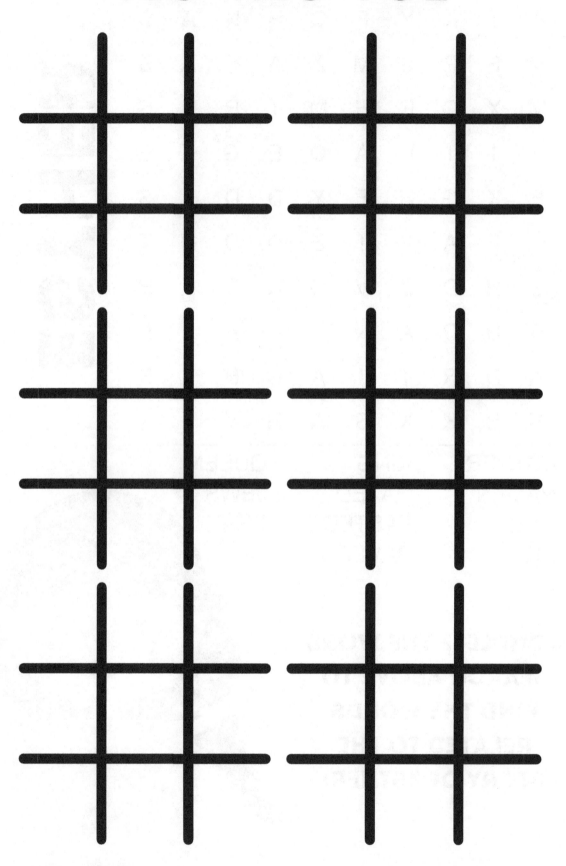

PLAYER ONE____   **PLAYER TWO____**

HIDDEN PICTURES

FIND THE PICTURES LISTED BELOW HIDDEN INSIDE THE PICTURE AND COLOR THEM WHEN YOU FIND THEM.

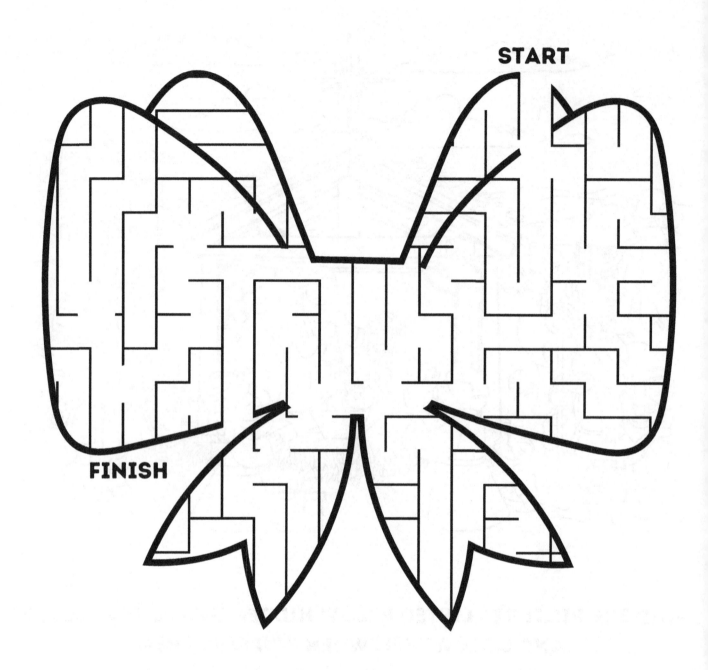

THE WISE MEN BROUGHT GIFTS TO JESUS. MAKE YOUR WAY THROUGH THE BOW MAZE ABOVE.

I CAN GIVE GIFTS TO JESUS

COLOR THE PICTURE OF BABY JESUS. WHAT "GIFTS" COULD YOU GIVE TO JESUS? IDEAS INCLUDE BEING KIND TO YOUR FAMILY, PRAYING, & GOING TO CHURCH.

```
E  Z  S  G  I  F  T  S  D  A
E  B  H  E  M  I  W  E  Y  M
N  E  E  J  I  U  O  G  L  R
M  T  P  E  F  B  R  J  S  O
A  H  H  S  T  R  S  O  T  Z
N  L  E  U  L  M  H  S  A  V
G  E  R  S  V  A  I  E  R  A
E  H  D  X  V  R  P  P  U  X
R  E  S  U  J  Y  P  H  K  Y
T  M  W  A  N  G  E  L  W  U
```

NATIVITY

MARY   ANGEL   JESUS
JOSEPH   BETHLEHEM STAR
MANGER   SHEPHERDS GIFTS
WORSHIP

COMPLETE THE WORD SEARCH ABOVE TO FIND THE WORDS RELATED TO THE STORY OF THE BIRTH OF JESUS.

SPOT THE DIFFERENCES

THE WISE MEN TRAVELED TO SEE JESUS & BROUGHT HIM GIFTS. SPOT THE SIX DIFFERENCE BETWEEN THE TWO PICTURES & CIRCLE THE DIFFERENCES IN THE BOTTOM PICTURE.

WE CAN FOLLOW JESUS' EXAMPLE & BE BAPTIZED. WE CAN BE BAPTIZED WHEN WE ARE EIGHT YEARS OLD.

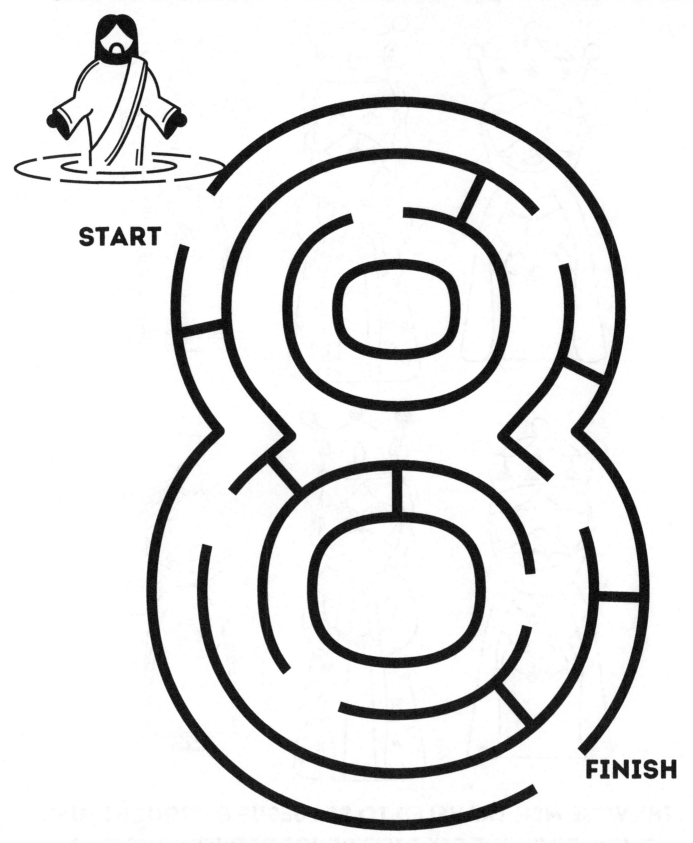

START

FINISH

IT'S GREAT TO BE 8!

WHICH ONE IS DIFFERENT?

JESUS IS THE GOOD SHEPHERD & KNOWS EACH ONE OF US.
HE WANTS US ALL TO COME UNTO HIM & BELIEVE. FIND THE
SHEEP THAT IS DIFFERENT FROM THE OTHERS AND COLOR IT.

JESUS TAUGHT US TO LOVE ONE ANOTHER. COLOR THE PICTURE ABOVE.

TIC-TAC-TOE

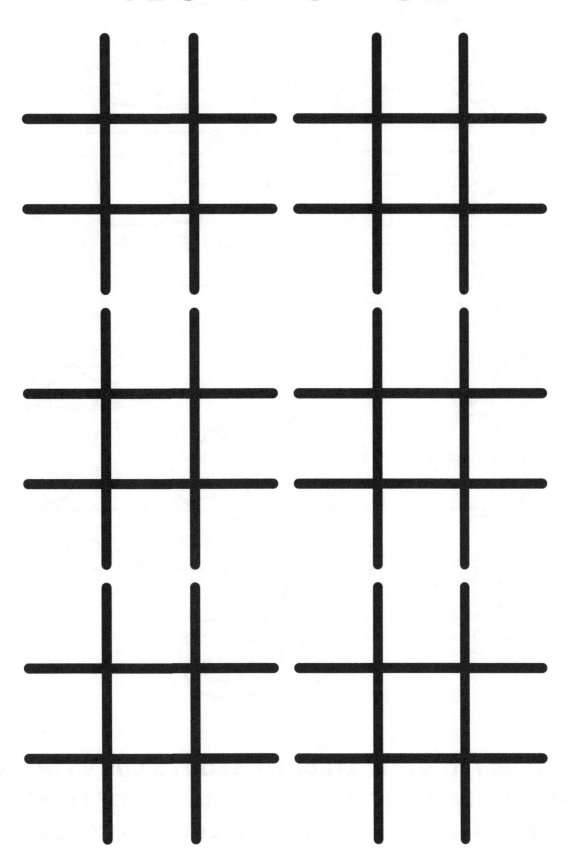

PLAYER ONE___   **PLAYER TWO___**

WHICH ONE IS DIFFERENT?

JESUS FED A MULTITUDE OF ABOUT 5,000 WITH FIVE
LOAVES & TWO FISHES. FIND THE BARREL OF FISHES THAT
IS DIFFERENT FROM THE OTHERS AND COLOR IT.

JESUS KNOWS YOU.

JESUS LOVES YOU.

COLOR THE PICTURE OF JESUS ABOVE.

CRACK THE CODE

KEY

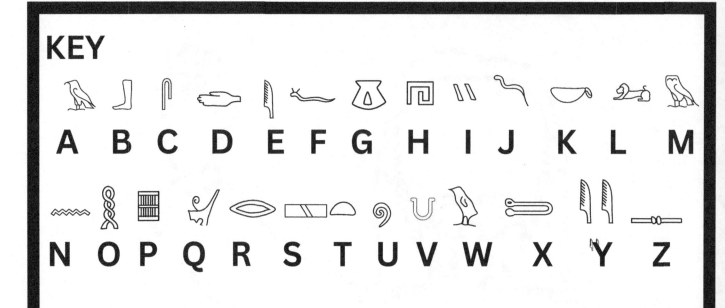

DECODE THIS TEACHING OF JESUS.

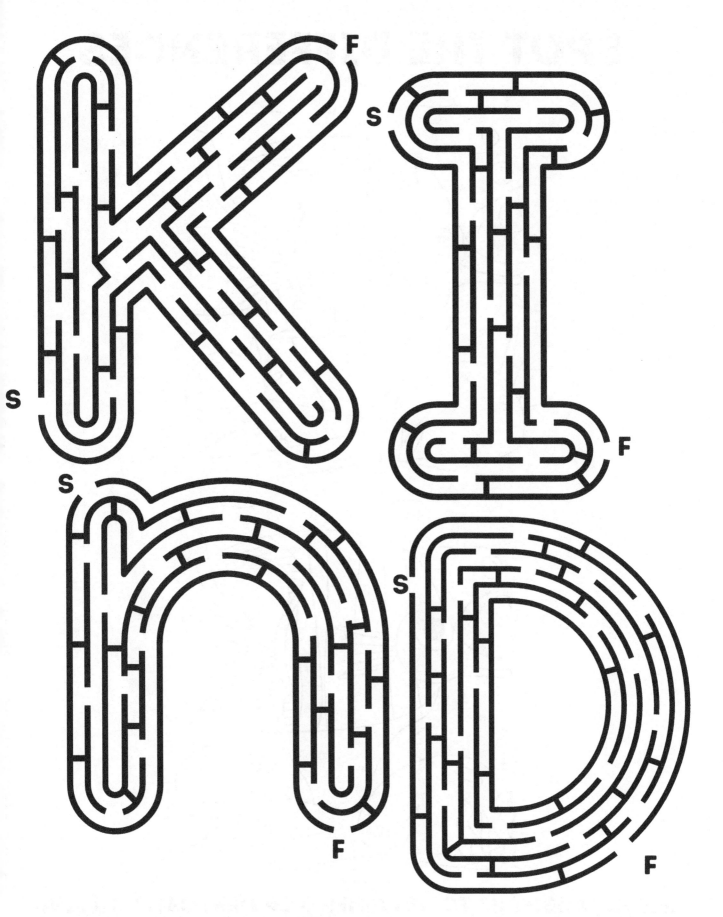

JESUS TAUGHT US TO BE KIND. MAKE YOUR WAY THROUGH THE FOUR MAZES ABOVE. THE START ("S") & FINISH ("F") ARE MARKED FOR YOU.

SPOT THE DIFFERENCES

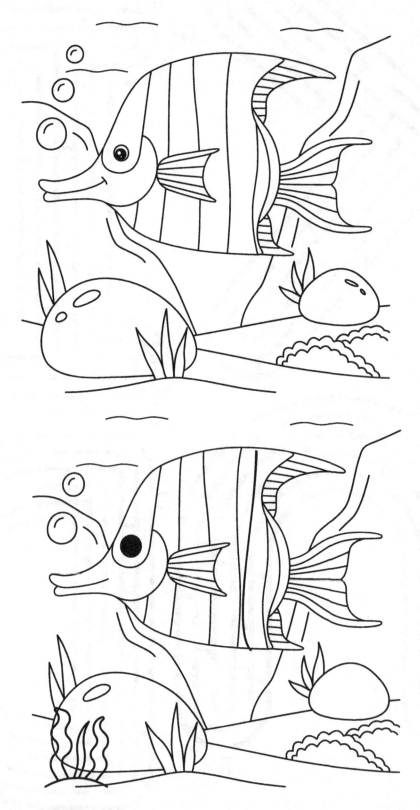

JESUS TAUGHT US TO BE FISHER'S OF MEN. CAN YOU FIND
THE DIFFERENCES BETWEEN THE TWO PICTURES ABOVE?
CIRCLE THE SIX DIFFERENCES IN THE BOTTOM PICTURE.

LET YOUR LIGHT SHINE

HOW MANY WORDS CAN YOU MAKE USING THE LETTERS ABOVE IN "LET YOUR LIGHT SHINE"?

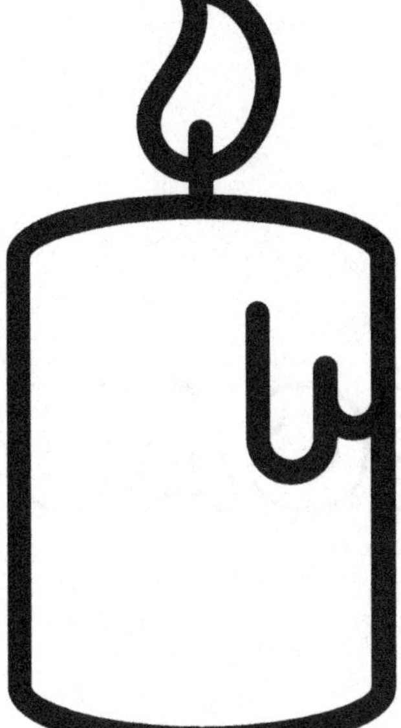

_____   _____

_____   _____

_____   _____

_____   _____

_____   _____

_____   _____

_____

_____

_____

_____

WE CAN LIVE AGAIN

BECAUSE OF JESUS

COLOR THE PICTURE ABOVE.

```
D  B  T  G  C  R  O  S  S  I
U  R  K  O  X  A  C  D  A  S
N  T  O  W  M  C  M  N  C  E
K  V  H  B  T  B  E  A  R  S
I  Y  F  O  E  D  S  G  A  S
N  P  O  J  R  E  K  Y  M  A
D  D  A  A  V  N  I  Q  E  V
F  P  G  I  S  M  S  X  N  I
T  W  L  E  N  W  N  M  T  O
K  Z  W  D  X  U  Q  B  X  R
```

JESUS

SACRAMENT	GARDEN	SAVIOR
PAIN	ROBE	THORNS
UNKIND	CROSS	TOMB
LIVES		

COMPLETE THE WORD SEARCH ABOVE TO FIND THE WORDS RELATED TO THE FINAL WEEK OF CHRIST'S LIFE.

SPOT THE DIFFERENCES

**SPOT THE SIX DIFFERENCES BETWEEN THE TWO PICTURES.
CIRCLE DIFFERENCES IN BOTTOM PICTURE.**

FINISH

START

WE CELEBRATE EASTER TO REMEMBER THE RESURRECTION OF JESUS CHRIST & HIS VICTORY OVER DEATH. WE ALSO REMEMBER HIS ATONEMENT THAT ALLOWS US TO REPENT & BE FORGIVEN. COMPLETE THE MAZE ABOVE.

TIC-TAC-TOE

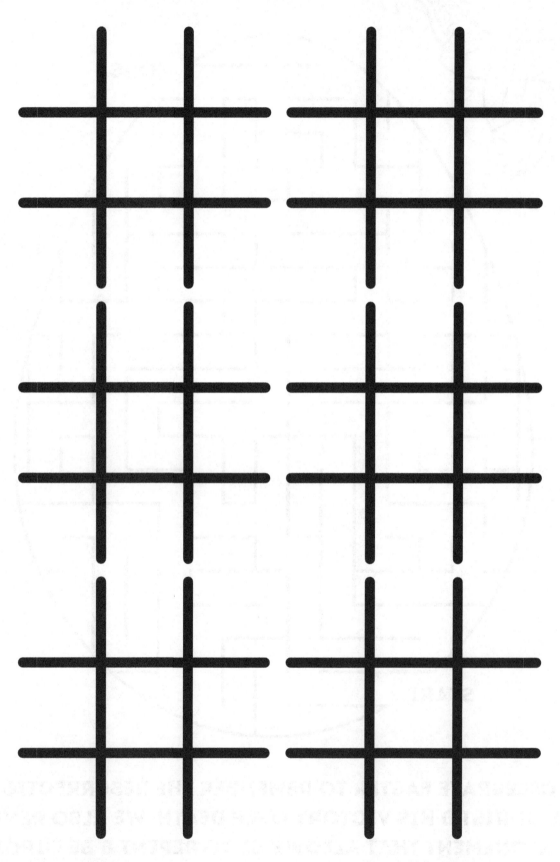

PLAYER ONE___   **PLAYER TWO___**

FRUIT OF THE SPIRIT

IN GALATIANS 5: 22-23, WE READ "BUT THE FRUIT OF THE SPIRIT IS LOVE, JOY, PEACE, LONGSUFFERING, GENTLENESS, GOODNESS, FAITH, MEEKNESS, TEMPERANCE"

COLOR THE FRUIT ABOVE.

THE APOSTLES LEAD THE CHURCH

FINISH

START

AFTER JESUS DIED, HIS APOSTLES LED THE CHURCH & DID MUCH MISSIONARY WORK. COMPLETE THE MAZE ABOVE AND HELP THE APOSTLE GET TO HIS DESTINATION.

HOW MANY DO YOU COUNT?

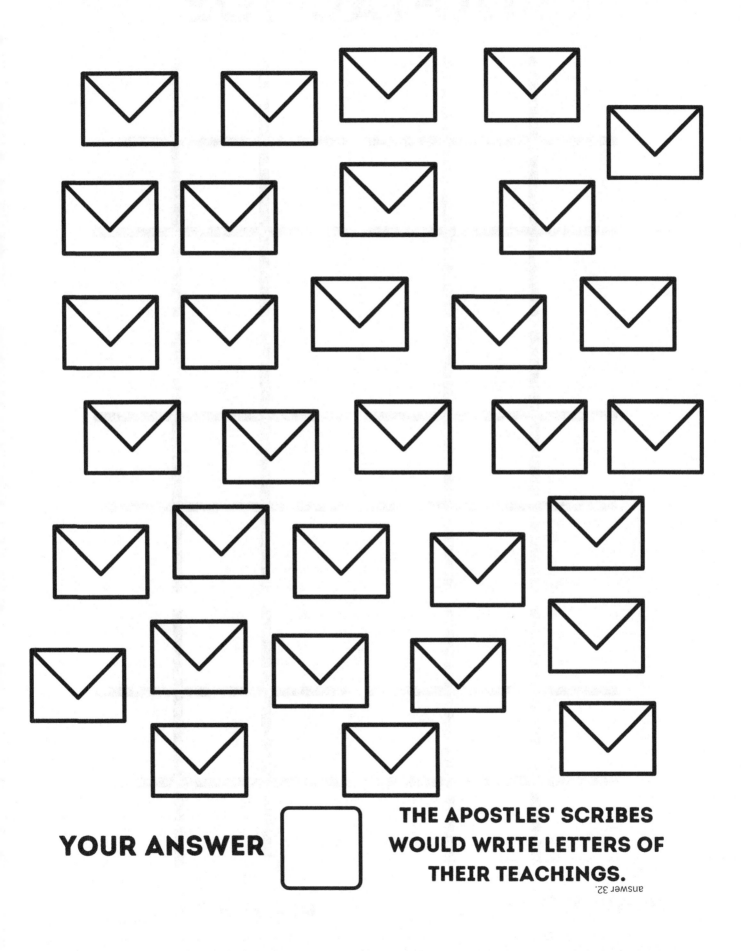

YOUR ANSWER

THE APOSTLES' SCRIBES WOULD WRITE LETTERS OF THEIR TEACHINGS.

answer 32.

TIC-TAC-TOE

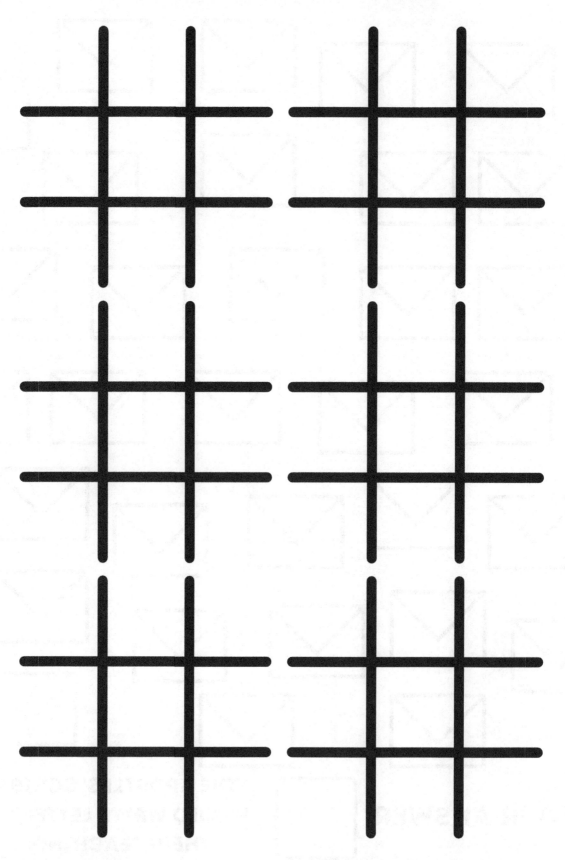

PLAYER ONE___   **PLAYER TWO___**

NEPHI WAS OBEDIENT

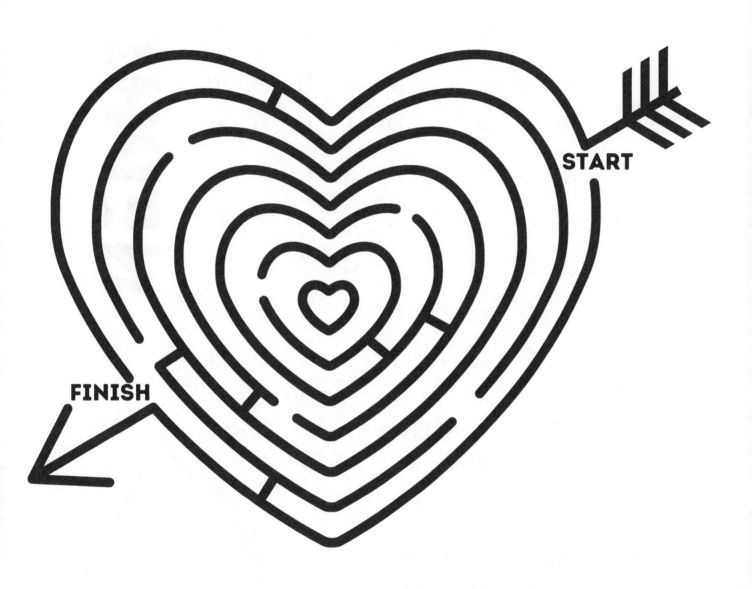

NEPHI WAS OBEDIENT & DID WHAT THE LORD COMMANDED. COMPLETE THE MAZE ABOVE.

```
M  H  W  E  X  W  Y  Y  R  W
H  T  E  H  R  T  R  F  A  J
B  R  O  T  H  E  R  S  V  M
T  A  W  N  S  M  V  B  O  W
L  V  N  E  P  H  I  P  N  N
S  E  Q  G  S  F  S  L  I  Y
X  L  H  V  T  N  I  A  Y  U
R  O  D  I  U  Z  O  T  P  E
Q  N  C  F  Q  P  N  E  S  J
G  Z  B  O  A  T  S  S  D  U
```

NEPHI

LEHI	NEPHI	VISION
TRAVEL	PLATES	BROTHERS
ROD	TREE	BOW
BOAT		

COMPLETE THE WORD SEARCH ABOVE TO FIND THE WORDS RELATED TO THE STORY OF NEPHI.

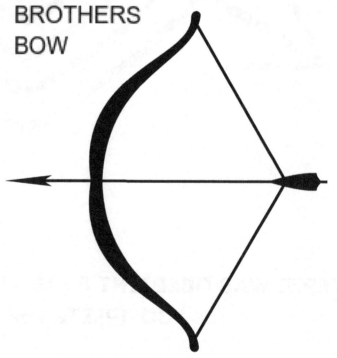

CRACK THE CODE

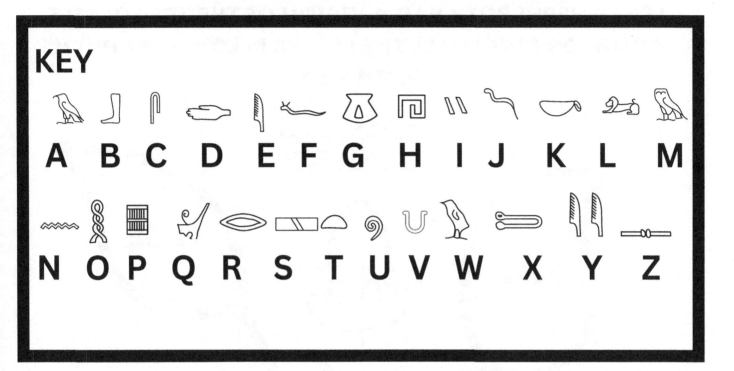

KEY

A	B	C	D	E	F	G	H	I	J	K	L	M

N	O	P	Q	R	S	T	U	V	W	X	Y	Z

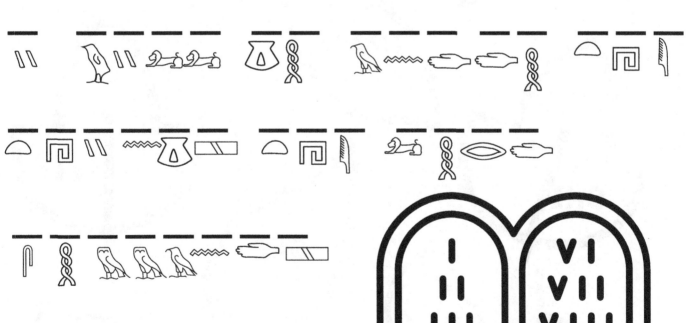

HELP DECODE NEPHI'S MESSAGE

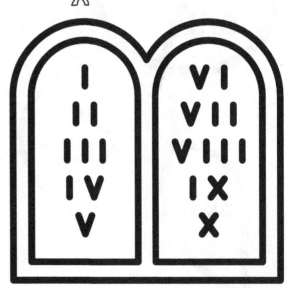

RHYME TIME

LEHI & NEPHI BOTH HAD A VISION OF THE TREE OF LIFE.
COLOR OR CIRCLE ALL THE LEAVES BELOW THAT RHYME
WITH TREE.

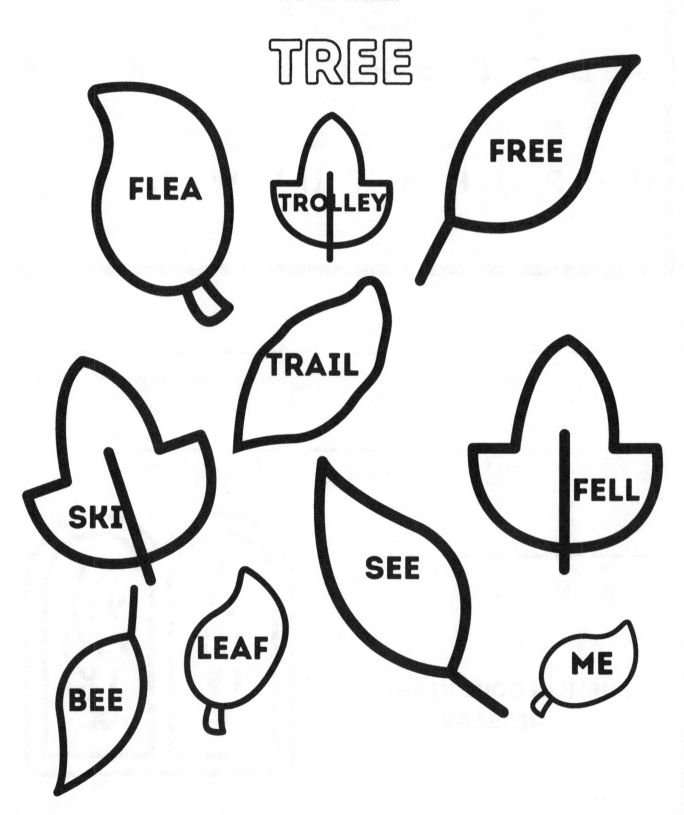

TIC-TAC-TOE

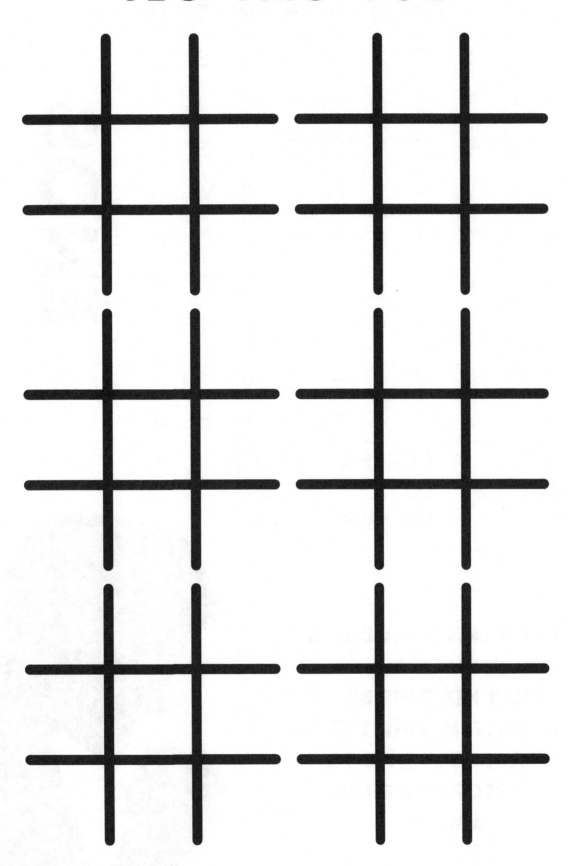

PLAYER ONE___   **PLAYER TWO___**

```
C  L  H  R  D  R  B  N  T  P
I  F  B  T  A  S  K  G  S  L
P  O  B  E  O  H  F  O  J  E
D  R  Z  T  N  K  D  D  S  A
O  G  A  S  L  O  V  E  W  L
G  I  X  Y  K  X  S  J  D  R
N  V  W  Y  E  P  R  R  Q  Z
L  E  A  I  S  R  Z  L  T  X
H  U  M  B  L  E  B  X  F  T
L  F  A  I  T  H  D  X  H  U
```

ENOS

ENOS	PRAYER	FAITH
FORGIVE	LOVE	ASK
PLEA	HUMBLE	GOD

ENOS PRAYED ALL DAY & ALL NIGHT & ASKED THAT HIS SINS BE FORGIVEN. FIND THE WORDS RELATING TO THE STORY OF ENOS ABOVE.

FIND THE RIGHT ENTRANCE

HELP ENOS FIND THE CORRECT ENTRANCE TO GET TO THE CENTER OF THE MAZE & FIND AN ANSWER TO HIS PRAYER.

FIND THE MATCH

CAN YOU FIND WHICH TWO BOYS PRAYING EXACTLY MATCH? CIRCLE OR COLOR THE PICTURES THAT MATCH.

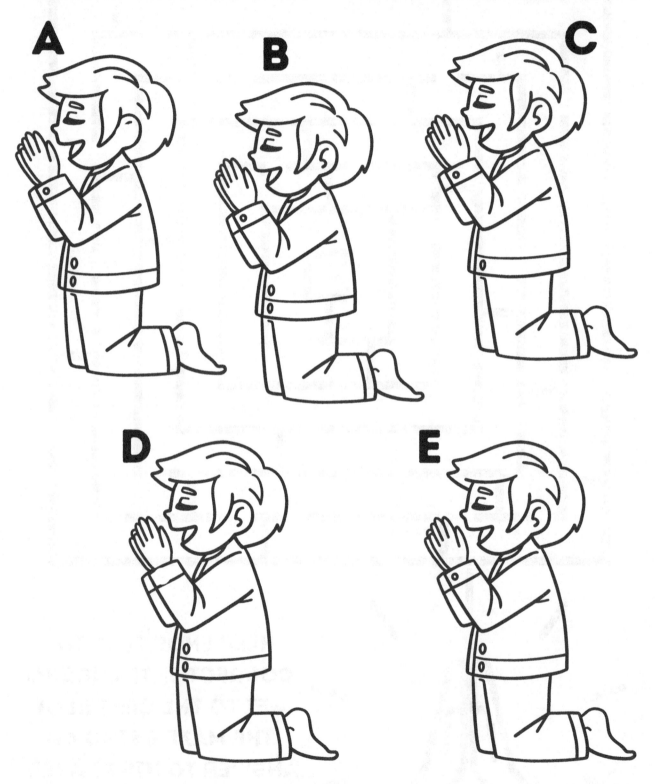

SERVING OTHERS SERVES GOD

HOW MANY WORDS CAN YOU MAKE USING THE LETTERS ABOVE FROM KING BENJAMIN'S TEACHINGS?

_____   _____

_____   _____

_____   _____

_____   _____

_____   _____

_____   _____

_____   _____

_____

_____

_____

TIC-TAC-TOE

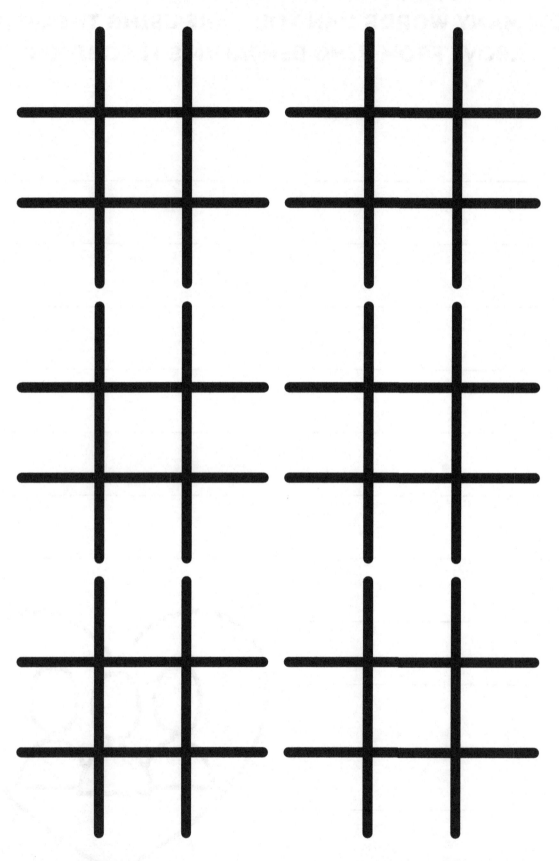

PLAYER ONE____   **PLAYER TWO____**

```
I  O  P  P  R  E  A  C  H  A
A  R  Q  C  H  R  I  S  T  B
X  Q  E  X  X  U  U  G  R  I
Y  B  X  P  C  S  F  D  O  N
W  I  C  K  E  D  A  L  M  A
T  S  R  V  I  N  C  G  E  D
Z  F  Y  M  N  N  T  N  Y  I
R  Z  P  X  N  S  G  A  P  C
N  K  M  O  S  I  A  H  J  P
W  V  L  V  M  Z  B  U  R  N
```

ABINADI

MOSIAH	ABINADI	PREACH
REPENT	KING	WICKED
CHRIST	BURN	ALMA

ABINADI PREACHED THE GOSPEL TO KING NOAH'S PEOPLE. NOAH WAS ANGRY WITH ABINADI & HIS PROPHECIES & HAD HIM BURNED. COMPLETE THE WORD SEARCH ABOVE RELATED TO THE STORY OF ABINADI.

ALMA TAUGHT ABINADI'S MESSAGE

HELP ALMA MAKE HIS WAY THROUGH THE MAZE TO THE WATERS OF MORMON TO BAPTIZE THE BELIEVERS.

WHICH ONE IS DIFFERENT?

AN ANGEL APPEARED TO ALMA THE YOUNGER & THE SONS OF
MOSIAH & TOLD THEM TO STOP PERSECUTING THE CHURCH.
FIND THE ANGEL ABOVE THAT IS DIFFERENT THAN THE OTHERS.

HIDDEN PICTURES

AMMON WAS A SON OF KING MOSIAH. AFTER HE REPENTED, HE PREACHED THE GOSPEL TO THE LAMANITES. AMMON SERVED THE LAMANITE KING LAMONI BY WATCHING HIS FLOCKS.

FIND THE FOLLOWING HIDDEN PICTURES AND CIRCLE OR COLOR THEM WHEN YOU FIND THEM.

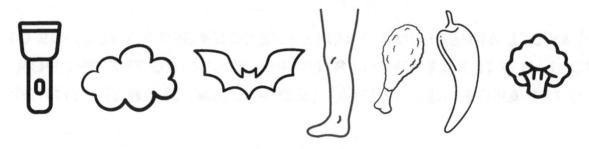

TIC-TAC-TOE

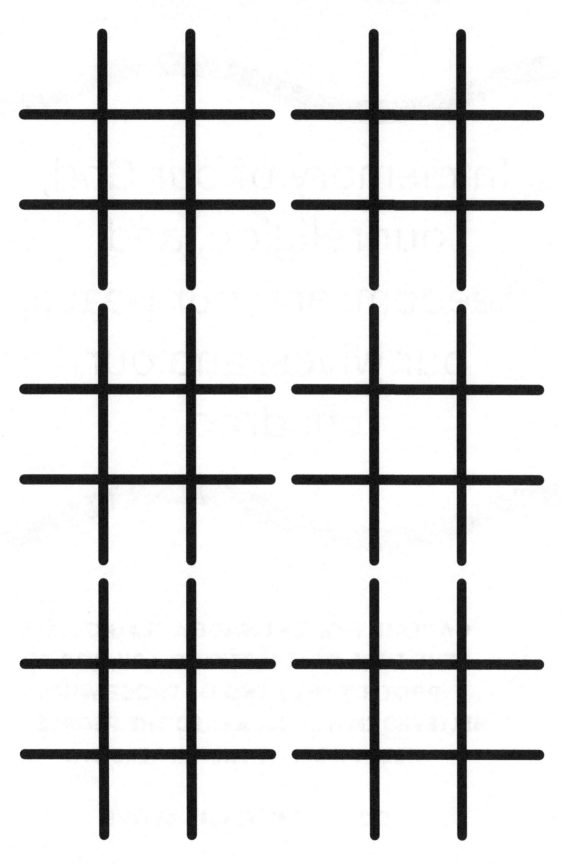

PLAYER ONE___　　　　　　　**PLAYER TWO___**

TITLE OF LIBERTY

In memory of our God, our religion, and freedom, and our peace, our wives, and our children

CAPTAIN MORONI MADE A FLAG CALLED "THE TITLE OF LIBERTY" TO ASK GOD TO PROTECT THE LAND OF THOSE WHO BELIEVED IN HIM. HE ASKED THE PEOPLE TO HELP PROTECT THEIR FREEDOM.

COLOR THE FLAG ABOVE.

```
W S H K S I D X D Z
C A T E A X Q R O R
F B R R L M X K G N
G R F R I C E B H K
I P C V I P A R M Y
B R A V E O L R H Q
H Z C X T V R I I L
N M O T H E R S N M
T C E T O R P S M G
Z N H N A M A L E H
```

STRIPLING WARRIORS

ARMY   STRIPLING   WARRIORS
HELAMAN   GOD   PROTECT
MOTHERS   BRAVE   MIRACLE

THE PEOPLE OF AMMON HAD PROMISED THEY WOULD NOT FIGHT AGAIN. THEIR SONS HAD NOT MADE THAT PROMISE & THEY WANTED TO HELP THE NEPHITE ARMY FIGHT FOR FREEDOM.

FIND THE WORDS RELATED TO THE STORY OF THE STRIPLING WARRIORS IN THE WORD SEARCH.

SAMUEL TOLD THE NEPHITES TO REPENT

SAMUEL THE LAMANITE TOLD THE NEPHITES THEY MUST REPENT.

HELP SAMUEL MAKE HIS WAY THROUGH THE MAZE & TO THE TOP OF THE WALL.

HOW MANY DO YOU COUNT?

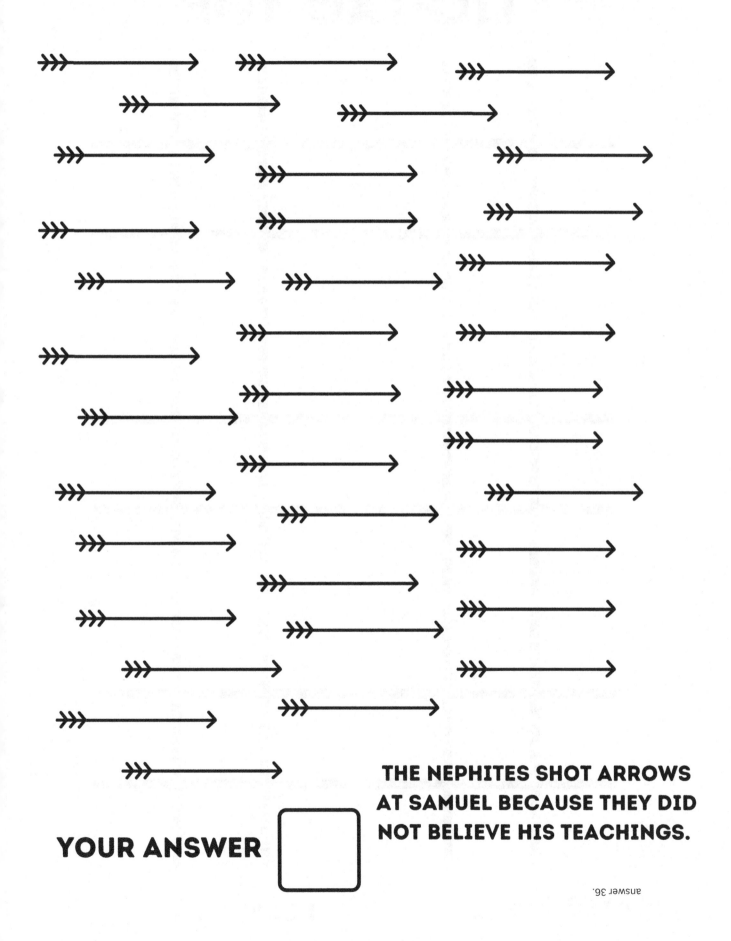

YOUR ANSWER

THE NEPHITES SHOT ARROWS AT SAMUEL BECAUSE THEY DID NOT BELIEVE HIS TEACHINGS.

answer 36.

TIC-TAC-TOE

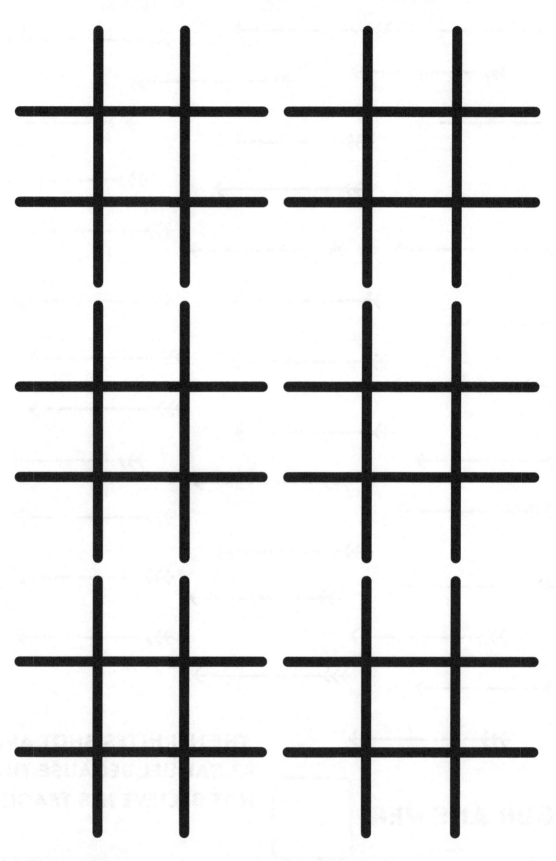

PLAYER ONE____   **PLAYER TWO____**

CHRIST VISITS THE NEPHITES

HELP THE NEPHITES MAKE THEIR WAY TO THE TEMPLE IN THE LAND BOUNTIFUL TO SEE THE RESURRECTED JESUS CHRIST.

CHRIST VISITS

```
W L Y V D P M T X C
L W U I A J O S A S
U P K S R H S I S N
G T Z I K G X R E L
T P R T N T U H L U
E E F S E V H C T H
E A M I S Q U R S A
F C T P S V M D O N
M E X W L R E P P D
N S E S S E L B A S
```

DARKNESS TEMPLE CHRIST
VISITS HANDS FEET
BLESSES APOSTLES PEACE

AFTER HIS RESURRECTION, CHRIST VISITED THE NEPHITES & TAUGHT & BLESSED THEM. HE CALLED 12 APOSTLES. COMPLETE THE WORD SEARCH ABOVE.

JESUS BLESSED THE CHILDREN

DRAW A PICTURE OF YOU & JESUS. WHAT WOULD YOU ASK HIM TO BLESS YOU WITH?

TRACE IT

JESUS APPEARED TO NEPHITES & TAUGHT THEM. TRACE THE PICTURE OF JESUS ABOVE.

RHYME TIME

JESUS TAUGHT THE NEPHITES HOW TO PRAY. CIRCLE ALL THE TEXT BUBBLES WITH WORDS INSIDE THEM THAT RHYME WITH PRAY.

TIC-TAC-TOE

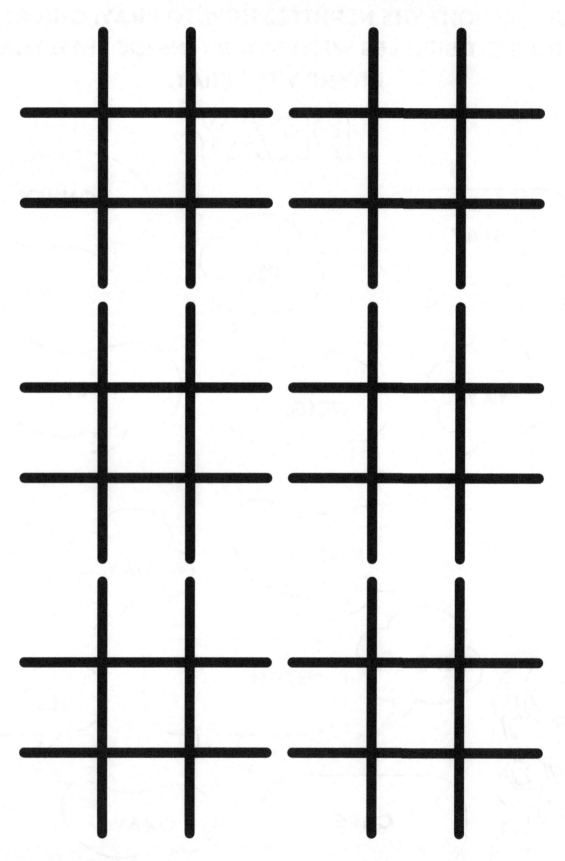

PLAYER ONE____   **PLAYER TWO____**

MORMON WROTE ABOUT JESUS

1   2   3

FIND THE RIGHT ENTRANCE TO THE MAZE TO MAKE IT TO THE END OF MAZE AND FIND A HIDING SPOT FOR THE GOLD PLATES.

```
Y C B K D Y T B R J
W I C K E D S K G J
M V I R S E B N F M
O H I D T F A E S P
R Y C A R M T P L L
O Y L N O O T H Y L
N P F R Y A L I V I
I Q M E E B E T Z H
F O Q I D D Z E D L
N E S I Q W Y S U A
```

NEPHITES

DESTROYED

NEPHITES	WICKED	MORMON
BATTLE	HILL	PLATES
HID	MORONI	DESTROYED

MORMON LED THE NEPHITES IN MANY BATTLES, BUT THEY WERE DESTROYED BECAUSE OF THEIR WICKEDNESS. COMPLETE THE WORD SEARCH ABOVE.

THE BROTHER OF JARED

HOW MANY WORDS CAN YOU MAKE USING THE LETTERS ABOVE IN THE WORDS "THE BROTHER OF JARED"?

_____   _____

_____   _____

_____   _____

_____   _____

_____   _____

_____   _____

_____   _____

_____   _____

_____

_____

CRACK THE CODE

KEY

HELP DECODE MORONI'S MESSAGE

TIC-TAC-TOE

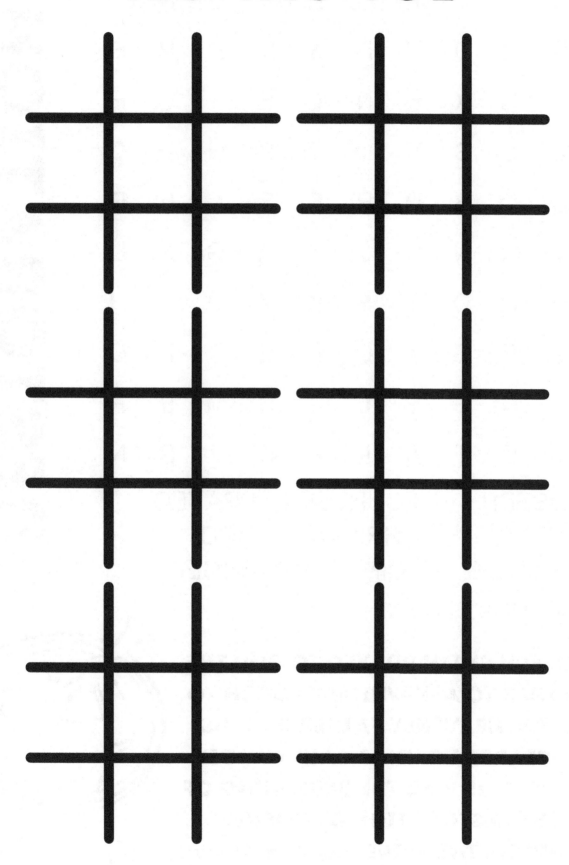

PLAYER ONE____   **PLAYER TWO____**

```
T H L X U H M U N X
R K D X P X M E R S
E G X E N L E I C H
E L S V O T P H P C
S O B D R E R L E R
J Q N U G I A G X U
M Q O I S K Y O T H
Z F G T O L E D P C
A N G E L J D M B P
S E T A L P G J P N
```

JOSEPH	FOURTEEN	PRAYED
TREES	CHRIST	GOD
CHURCH	JOIN	ANGEL
PLATES		

JOSEPH SMITH PRAYED TO GOD THE FATHER TO ASK WHICH CHURCH TO JOIN. HEAVENLY FATHER & JESUS APPEARED TO HIM & SAID TO JOIN NONE. THIS WAS THE BEGINNING OF THE RESTORATION OF GOSPEL. COMPLETE THE WORD SEARCH ABOVE.

ANGEL MORONI APPEARED TO JOSEPH SMITH

START

FINISH

THE ANGEL MORONI APPEARED TO JOSEPH SMITH AND TOLD HIM WHERE TO FIND THE GOLD PLATES. MAKE YOUR WAY THROUGH THE MAZE.

TIC-TAC-TOE

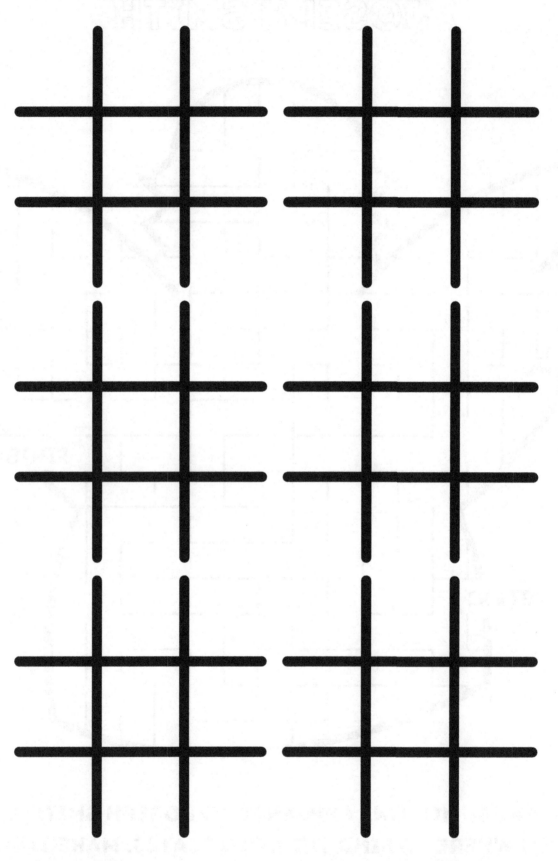

PLAYER ONE____   **PLAYER TWO____**

FIND THE MATCH
CAN YOU FIND WHICH TWO WAGONS EXACTLY MATCH?
CIRCLE OR COLOR THE PICTURES THAT MATCH.

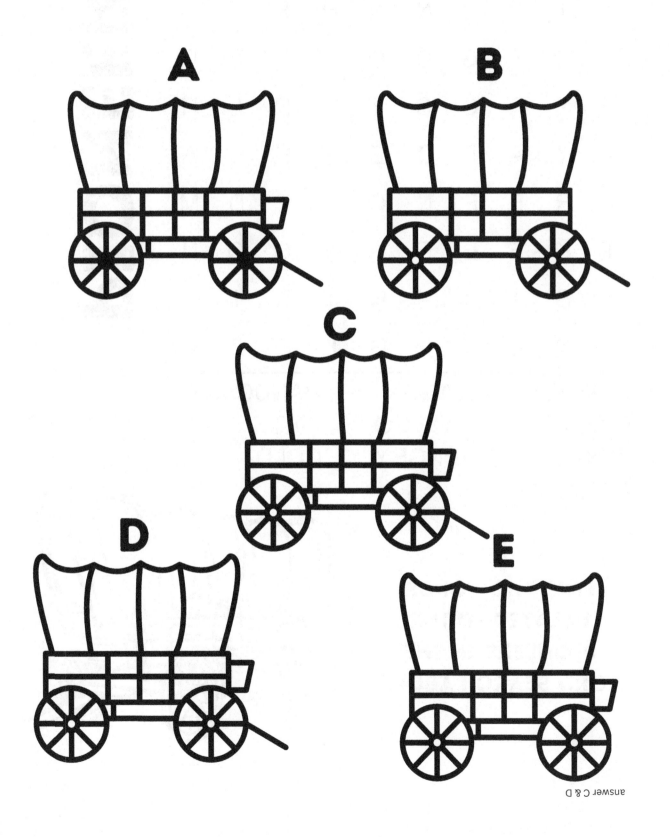

answer C & D

```
B V F A I T H H V B
F B O O V U A N Q R
X I H I N N H F T I
P Q F G D O L L Y G
H Y R C O I V R L H
A Y A F D Z J K S A
V R E E N O I P D M
T K E E E W A G O N
T S I W K N I L I D
X N E X O D L O C L
```

PIONEERS

PIONEER	WAGON	HANDCART
OXEN	NAUVOO	FAITH
ZION	HUNGRY	COLD
BRIGHAM		

**FIND THE WORDS
RELATED TO THE
PIONEERS IN THE
WORD SEARCH ABOVE.**

HOW MANY DO YOU COUNT?

YOUR ANSWER

THE PIONEERS ATE BUFFALO &
USED BUFFALO CHIPS TO
BURN IN THEIR FIRES.

answer 78.

WHICH WAY TO ZION?

HELP THE PIONEERS PICK THE CORRECT PATH TO GET TO ZION.

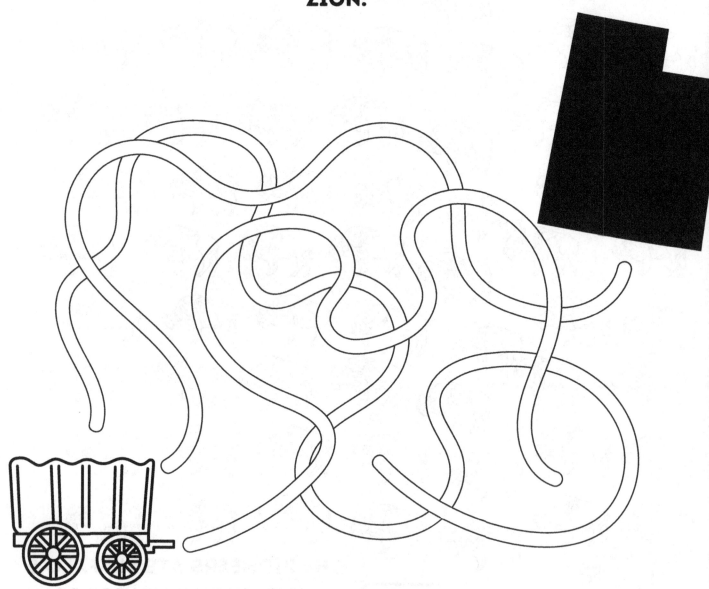

TRACE IT

I LOVE TO SEE THE TEMPLE

TRACE THE SALT LAKE TEMPLE ABOVE.

I AM GRATEFUL

DRAW A PICTURE OF SOMETHING YOU ARE GRATEFUL FOR. YOU CAN LIST ADDITIONAL THINGS ON THE LINES BELOW.

_____

_____

_____

IF YOU ENJOYED THIS BOOK, MAKE SURE TO LEAVE A REVIEW.

ALSO, MAKE SURE TO CHECK OUT OUR OTHER BOOKS!

FOLLOW US ONLINE!

@LATTER.DAY.DESIGNS

LATTER-DAY DESIGNS

Made in the USA
Las Vegas, NV
06 March 2024

86813221R00072